Anni & Carsten Sennov

GET YOUR POWER BACK NOW!
The Energy Guide for Children and Young Adults

good adventures publishing

Get Your Power Back Now!
The Energy Guide for Children and Young Adults

©2014, Anni & Carsten Sennov and Good Adventures Publishing
First edition, third impression
Set with Cambria
Layout: Anni & Carsten Sennov - www.good-adventures.dk
Cover design: Michael Bernth - www.monovoce.dk
Author photo: Semko Balcerski - www.semko.dk

Original title in Danish:
Tag din kraft tilbage nu! - Energiguide for børn & unge

Translated into English by: Sue Jonas and David Tugwell

ISBN 978-87-92549-46-4

Contents

Thanks

Thanks to our four children Sandra, Ask, Julian and Astrid, and to Astrid's friends Ditte and Cecilie for giving us positive feedback on this book.

It's great to know that we have written a book that has really hit the spot for you young people who are all so different – that means there is hope that a lot of other youngsters will also like this book.

Welcome!

Most of you children and young adults are very clear in the way you express yourselves compared to others, both when you speak and when you use body language and your energy without actually having to say anything. Often one doesn't have to know you at all to know what you think about things. It's so obvious just by looking at you to know whether you are interested in something, or completely indifferent to or bored by it, or if you are happy, angry or sad.

When you are very direct, as many of you are, then it should be really easy for most adults to communicate with you, but unfortunately, not all adults are as direct and honest in the way they express themselves as you are. They aren't always completely honest with themselves. All too often they don't dare to look the truth in the eye and accept life as it is. So it can be extremely provocative for them to have you stand up and tell them that it isn't really so difficult to decide to do something to change the situation. It is interesting that children are often quicker to realize that there is something wrong in their parents' relationships than the parents themselves. So often, they are not surprised when their parents end up getting a divorce.

With your direct way of being you must unfortunately be prepared for the roles sometimes being reversed, meaning that you behave in a more adult, responsible and insightful way than some adults. Maybe you actually end up giving the adults good advice, and it is of course wonderful that children and adults can support each other. However, as a child or young person you must not forget who has lived the longest, and therefore who has had the most experience of life. Just imagine if adults did not share their life experience with you, then all children and young people throughout the world would have to make the very same mistakes as they did in the olden days and we would perhaps still be living in caves. Worst of all, they would probably not have developed the computers, mobile phones or iPads that many of you spend so much time on every day.

This is the reason that we decided to write this energy guide, to share a certain type of knowledge with you that not many parents and adults are able to explain, either to themselves or to you. Energy is our biggest interest and we work with it every day, which makes it easy for us to explain how it works to others.

In this book we will clearly explain what happens on an invisible level between people when there could sometimes be a problem between you and those you love most, as well as with the many other people you may encounter in your everyday lives. So when things sometimes look really difficult, it could in fact just take a simple thing to change the situation, if only you knew what to do and how.

So if you are interested in learning how you can master your own energy when you are with other people, or if sometimes you feel lonely, then you have picked up the right book and we have tried to make it as short, simple and easy to understand as possible.

Happy reading!

Happy energy greetings from

Anni & Carsten Sennov

Children and young adults
know about energy

As a young person, it is generally much easier for you than it is for your parents to understand energy. It is often faster and more effective to use your own power and strength to deal with energy than if your parents have to control your energy for you. The fact is that many of you are born with an increased and much stronger personal energy and have a more developed understanding of the energy-related and technological developments taking place on Earth right now than your parents do.

You are the adults of the future and therefore you have an energy within you that will extend a little further out into the future than your parents' energy. Your parents' energy, in turn, is supposed to be used at this particular moment in time so that they can advise and guide you youngsters, so that you can become really good citizens of the world... and good citizens are always trying to live their lives in a responsible, balanced and successful way, for the benefit of themselves and others.

So all you young people, start now on sorting out your energy every morning, at lunchtime and at night as well as after you have been with other people at school or at home. This is what our four children have been doing for years, and now that three of them are almost adults, and two of them have left home, they still sort out their energy. In fact it is as natural for them to keep an eye on their energy as it is to brush their teeth or to eat and sleep.

Exchange of energy

There are three types of energy exchange between people, and if you are always aware of which of these three types are operating when you are with others, then you will quickly be a master at balancing your own energy and coping well when you are interacting with others.

You may be in perfect balance in your relationship with some people because you support and help each other equally and want to do good things for each other, and here you both of you will be happy.

Or you might also choose to volunteer to help others just because you want to do something nice for them, and because it makes you happy to do it. They may not have the energy to help you in return or to give you anything back, but you feel great because they are people that you like and they are happy that you are helping them.

And finally there are the energy thieves – people who want something from you, and who are unhappy no matter how much you help them or give them. In fact, spending time with them and trying to help them will put you in a bad mood. Maybe they will even take something from you without permission, and then you will be in an extremely bad mood. So stay far away from them.

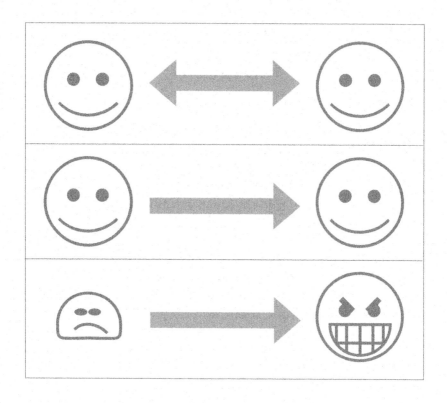

9

Do you think about other people too much?

Maybe you think about a good friend or a girlfriend or boyfriend all the time, either because you really like them or because you want to help them and worry about them. If so, you risk giving them too much attention. This increases their energy level so that other people will find them more interesting than usual to be with.

By doing this, the result might be that suddenly they don't have as much time to be with you as you would really like. This is because if you think about them all the time, they will always have your energy around them, and they will then not need to be with you as much to have some of your energy.

You could say that they are living so well on the attention that you are giving them that they don't really feel if they are missing you or not because as humans we usually only miss those who matter to us if they aren't around and we can't feel their energy because they are busy with something else.

So the result of giving your best friends and/or your girlfriend or boyfriend or other people a lot of attention by thinking about them all the time, especially when you're apart, is that often, without even knowing it, they go around with twice as much energy and attractiveness, while you are sitting at home waiting to hear from them and feeling completely forgotten and empty inside. This is because your own energy and attention has been laid on top of their energy as an extra-strong energy field, so they suddenly seem much more appealing and interesting than they might actually be.

Try to think back, as you have probably experienced this more than once, just like a lot of other people.

Most of us would really like to be with people with strong charisma and lots of energy to share, and of course it is okay for energy-rich people to go around with their own charisma and attractiveness. However, it's definitely not okay if they go around with both their own energy and your energy too, and that, in the meantime, you sit powerless at home and feel forgotten, while they are using your energy to have fun and live life to the full.

It is also the case that they can attract a lot of additional benefits that would otherwise have been split between two people, them and you. For if they go around with two people's energies, even though they are not really all their own, then they are able to attract the benefits and attention which are really for two people. You will probably not get any benefit from this even though you have been supporting them with all your attention.

So you should always keep your energy with you and let others benefit from it when they are with you. If you are a really nice, fun and loving person, then they will want to be with you a lot, and then you can get to control when you are together, so you don't always have to wait for when it suits them to be with you. In good friendships and relationships there needs to be a balance between the two sides.

How to help your friends

If you have some really good friends and/or a girlfriend or boy-friend or a family member that you want to support in a certain situation, then you have probably already guessed that by think-ing about them a lot and sending them masses of good thoughts you can help them to succeed in an amazing way. This will work if they have exams or are playing in an important football match, or if they are going to hospital, and so on.

After their exams or football match, it is important that you remember to draw all your energy back towards you so that you get the benefit of it yourself. Otherwise others will still have your energy available to them, which they can use as they please, and that is perhaps not the way you would use the energy yourself.

Unpleasant and annoying people

If you go around thinking a lot about people who are unpleasant or do ugly and hateful things to others, then they will get a lot of extra attention and energy from you that they do not deserve to have. Maybe you will also be going around building up fears about what they might do.

Thinking about someone or something bad all the time can, unfortunately, lead to you attracting bad experiences and people into your life because with your thoughts you are giving energy to something that is bad and suddenly the thing you feared will happen, because you have given them a lot of energy and attention.

It's like when you are afraid to walk alone in the dark after watching a scary movie, because you are then giving all your power and energy to the darkness and to things you can't see.

If instead you imagined that you were watching the movie without the sound, then all of a sudden it wouldn't seem so scary, and it would be much easier for you to hold on to your energy and get rid of your fear, which is actually just energy expressed in an in-appropriate way, so that nothing and nobody else can control it.

You can do the same with unpleasant and annoying people, and instead of listening to all their negative talk, you can begin to think about something positive, then they will have no power over you and your energy.

Many youngsters often make trouble just to get attention, simply because they are bored and maybe not getting enough attention and love at home, or because there are problems at home. Often these troublemakers are just lonely and neglected youngsters who, in their own unfortunate way, are just trying to get adult attention. There is rarely anything malicious about them. So if you just occasionally show them a little care and respect by talking to them and telling them in a positive way that you don't like the things they are doing, then they will usually stop being so annoying.

However, it is not just young people who can be really annoying to the people around them and create a lot of turmoil. Adults can be like that too, especially if they are not being intellectually challenged or because they do not have something exciting to do at work or in their free time. People like this can be a nightmare to work with if you are an adult.

At school it is of course the responsibility of the teachers to control annoying students along with the children's parents, but the class can also get involved in solving the problem. Here it will always help things if you choose to draw all your energy back from your annoying classmates, otherwise there is a risk that they will fill the classroom with their anxiety and frustration and this will damage both your concentration and your learning opportunities.

It doesn't actually make any difference whether you give other people positive or negative attention, or whether you send them good or bad thoughts, because thoughts are energy and can act just like fuel for a car or a moped. The more fuel or attention you fill them with, the longer they can run and the more damage they can do if they aren't in balance. So it is much better to totally ignore unpleasant and annoying people, just as you should avoid watching horror movies if they make you scared.

You can't ignore unpleasant and annoying people just by keeping away from them. You also need to ignore them with your thoughts by completely forgetting to think about them, as if they didn't exist in your world. This avoids them picking you as a possible victim for their nastiness and teasing.

What you should do

Imagine in your mind's eye that you are sending everyone else's energy back to them and you are drawing all your own energy back to yourself.

The more often you do this, the better you will be at holding on to your own energy. So if you do it at least in the morning, at lunchtime and at night, and also when you have been with your friends and family or at school or at a party, then you are well on the way to doing yourself a lot of good.

It only takes two minutes and you can do it anytime, anywhere.

Say the following sentence out loud or to yourself, or see it in your mind's eye, and if you can't see it in your mind's eye, just repeat the sentence as many times as you can or have time for. It is better to do it just twice than not to do it at all:

I am now drawing all my personal energy back to myself in completely purified form, from all people, places and situations, and I am now sending everyone else's energy out of my energy field and back to them in the same form as they originally sent it to me.

A bad start to the day

Everyone, whether they are children or adults, has the experience, once in a while, of starting the day in a really awful way. Maybe you are tired and grumpy in the morning because you have slept badly or because you have been thinking about something that annoys you.

Then when you get to school or work, everything continues to be really unpleasant, because others can read all your thoughts and feelings very clearly, whether you think it's possible or not.

Some people can sense your grumpiness and others can just see straightaway that you are in a bad mood, even if you are trying to hide it. So most happy people will keep themselves away from you until you are in a better mood, without being able to explain why. Those people who get a kick out of conflict and trouble will be happy to get close to you because they can sense that they might have the chance to sneak some extra energy from you because you are tired and in a bad mood and can't keep proper control of your own energy.

So if are you tired, irritated or grumpy, think this thought as many times as you can:

I am happy and everything good is coming to me.

This will stop you from attracting negative attention from others, whether it's at school, during sports or at home. This will also stop you getting into trouble or being accused of something you haven't done, just because you are in a slightly worse mood than usual and are therefore not as aware of what is happening around you as you normally are.

Do you give too much of yourself to others?

You can't love too much, but you can have so much energy and power and such a huge desire to help others that you totally overwhelm them with your love, attention and help, because they can't contain as much attention and care at one time as you can.

This may be because they don't have nearly as much energy as you. Their energy reservoir may be much smaller than yours, so there will be flooding everywhere if you try to help them by filling their reservoir with extra energy. This might be true even if they have asked you for help themselves. So sometimes it might turn out that people get angry even when you have just helped them the best you could, because they just can't contain the large amount of energy and power that you have given them.

A person with lots of energy has the power and strength to help many people, but there aren't many youngsters who have the chance to use up all their surplus energy helping a lot of people. So they often have to burn their energy up in sports and hobbies that they really love, and in that way they won't risk over-filling other people with their excess energy.

Unless you choose to burn off all your excess energy by doing sport or something else that you are really interested in, you must be very careful to try to share out your excess energy amongst as many different people as possible during the day and the week. Also, remember to always draw all your energy and attention back to yourself when you are no longer with others, and never give your friends and family, even your parents, more attention than they can tolerate. Also be aware that you have to experiment to find out how much attention other people can bear to have from you, without it becoming so strong that they can't handle it. You will get tips about how to do this in the next chapter.

How to do it

It is easy enough to see or hear whether other people are getting angry because you are trying to help them more than they can bear, as they will constantly complain and be deeply dissatisfied, or else they will become mean and sarcastic.

When it comes to people who really would like to have more of your energy without having to spend time with you, watch out and see if they don't suddenly start to behave in a different way than they normally would. If they suddenly start to become extraordinarily successful and completely forget about you, then it's worth drawing all your energy back to yourself and sending all their energy back to them.

It may also be that they start to change their behavior just by being near you, and this can sometimes be clearly seen by the fact that some people become very self-absorbed and start talking at a very loud volume, while others may suddenly be able to do a whole load of things that they wouldn't normally be able to do.

Extra energy which does not really belong to the person can show itself in many ways. Notice, for example, whether the person suddenly starts doing extraordinary things which they wouldn't be able to do normally and feel whether it is actually your energy that they are running on. If it is your energy that is being used, then you must immediately start to draw all your energy back as we described in the chapter *What you should do.*

Are you easily influenced by others?

If you are very sensitive it can be hard for you to be with other people who are coarse and negative in their way of being, whether they are children or adults. If you don't take extra care to protect yourself energetically, so that their thoughts and unpleasant way of speaking don't affect you, then you could easily end up with an unpleasant feeling, even when they are no longer near you.

Maybe you have already tried to send all their bad thoughts and unpleasant ways of speaking back to them and it hasn't worked properly. Instead, you could try to transform their negative energy into positive energy that can benefit you.

As an important ground rule when working with energy, remember that you must never open up to let other people's bad energy come into your energy field to get access to your energy. However, since their negative energy is floating everywhere in the air around you, and the people themselves don't want to have anything to do with their own bad energy, then you are within your rights to use all this energy to create something positive that will benefit you.

Imagine in your mind's eye that all the bad energy that others are sending in your direction or that they are filling the room with is changing from being negative and dark to being positive, bright and happy, so that it is you who is benefitting from it. Also, imagine how the energy is settling around you and acting as extra strength and creating a more powerful energy field for you.

In fact it is so easy that you'll find it difficult to believe, but the best thing is that it actually works!

Learn to stand on your own two feet

If there is something you really want, then things can often succeed more easily if there are a number of you working together. For example, you have a much greater chance of winning a football match if everyone on the team can agree to discuss things and make a plan about how to tackle the situation together.

On the other hand, it is a sign of weakness to get together in a group to bully and bother someone who is not in the group, no matter what the reason may be. It shows that the individual members of the group can't stand alone in relation to the person who is outside the group, and so who is really the weakest?

All young people are rehearsing, each in their own way, to become adults, because when you are an adult you should be able to manage yourself and stand on your own two feet. After all, you can't take your friends with you to work every day. So it is really good for you to learn to stand on your own two feet at an early age and be able to entertain yourself. So it's best that you don't get too bored in your own company, as then you risk boring others when you are with them, which is going to be a problem unless you have an agreement that they are the only ones who need to bring good energy and come up with lots of ideas when you are together.

It is also really important for you to have some good friends who don't share exactly the same views and who don't have the same upbringing as you. It can teach you how to work well with people who live and think in a different way from you.

All people on this Earth are different and there are very few people who do not feel a bit different from everyone else. In fact it would be really strange if everyone behaved in exactly the same way, as then we would all be the same and we would quickly get bored in each other's company. It is all these differences that help to make our lives exciting and challenging, and so it is important for you to find the strength, both in yourself and in your relationships with other people, to be who you really are.

Be yourself as you are inside

Don't try to imitate your friends because you think they are smarter or tougher than you feel you are inside. Perhaps they are only being tough because they want to make an impression on other people, including you. So when you are relaxed and being yourself, they will be able to feel that you are completely honest in your way of being and that there is nothing about you that they can't trust. So then they can easily be themselves when they are with you, without constantly having to think about what you might say about them afterwards to other people.

Deep down everyone would prefer to be popular by being themselves completely and utterly, instead of pretending that they are a different person from the one they really are.

Do you have too little energy?

If you are completely out of energy, think about what you've done, where you've been and who you've been with.

If you feel out of energy after sitting all day in front of the computer, then go out and get some fresh air and drink a lot of water. This can help to liven up your body. Otherwise, do some physical exercise and dance a little, or go for a run, as that can give you extra energy too.

When you sit for a long time in front of the computer or the TV, or you have your mobile phone and your iPad on your lap, then you are exposing yourself to radiation which is definitely not good for your body and your brain. So you should sleep as far away as you can from your computer, mobile phone or other electronic equipment. That way you will get a better and more refreshing night's sleep. Talk to your parents about what types of electronic protection you can use to reduce the radiation from all the electronic equipment you have at home, as there are many options available on the market today.

If you have ever slept outdoors, then you will know that you generally feel much more refreshed in the morning after sleeping outside all night than if you had slept indoors, and this is not only because of the fresh air. It is also due to the fact that you are sleeping well away from the radiation from your computer and mobile phone, etc.

If you get tired or irritable from being in certain places, it may be because some unpleasant things have happened in there and that the energy from those events is still hanging in the air and this is affecting you. As much as possible, avoid going to these places again, as it is not your job to clean up other people's bad energy.

If however your tiredness is due to being with people who don't give anything to you or to the group, but instead take away your energy, read about how to handle the situation in the chapter *What you should do* earlier in this book.

Do you have too much energy?

If you have an extraordinarily large amount of energy, then you can share your surplus energy with others as we wrote about in the chapter *How to help your friends*. But you should always remember to draw all your energy back to you when they have had all they need to get them through a particular situation. Also, remember to draw all your energy back to yourself if you can clearly see and feel that they can't bear to receive more without becoming very focused on themselves.

If there is a balance between your energy and your friends' energy, and both or all of you have lots of excess energy, then there is no point in giving energy to each other, as why would you need extra energy if you already have too much? So instead, find something positive to use your excess energy on which can benefit others who maybe need a helping hand.

There are always plenty of places you can help if you want to. But it's important that you use your surplus energy on something that you're comfortable with, otherwise you run the risk that your joy in helping others will soon disappear.

If you have so much energy that you can't control it, and it is expressed in an inappropriate way, then we would recommend that you put extra focus on first drawing all your energy back to you from the people, places and situations where you have used your energy inappropriately. Always remember to clean the energy before bringing it back. You can do that by imagining that you are running the energy through a cleansing filter before you let it come into your energy field.

Then you should draw all your energy back from all other people, places and situations, and here it is also important that you remember to clean the energy before you use your thoughts to draw it into your energy field.

Then take a few deep breaths, preferably outdoors, in the fresh air.

Finally, you then have to decide what you want to use all your energy on by trying to feel deep down if there is something you are really passionate about and which you really would like to use a lot of energy on.

Maybe you want to learn to play an instrument, to act, or do hip hop? Or maybe you're mad about motocross riding and want to feel the speed and excitement under your skin? It might also be that you are passionate about helping other people even if you aren't an adult yet. Who says you have to be an adult to start something big in life? Today it's so simple to spread your message to the whole world via the Internet if you have a good idea or something really interesting you want to share with others, or if you sing like an angel. All you have to do is record a video of yourself or others on your mobile phone and upload it onto YouTube. If you say or do something brilliant you will get lots of positive feedback, and if it is something not so good then no one will want to look at it. It's that easy!

It may be the case that you can't figure out how to express your energy in a sensible and balanced way when you are with other people, but that doesn't mean that you have a lot of bad energy in you. It means instead that you just don't know how to handle your own energy and you need help and guidance to change the situation. If this energy guide can't help you with this or at least help you a little bit along the way, we recommend that you have a chat with some adults to see if they have some good ideas on how you can start using your energy in a positive and satisfying way. Talk to your parents, but also to other adults such as your teachers and your friends' parents or your neighbours, as it can often be interesting and instructive to hear what they have to say. Since they will certainly have lived their lives differently from your parents, they will also have other types of life experience to share that are exactly what you may need to hear to move forward in your life in a really positive way.

Always clean up after yourself when you leave

To be polite and respectful to other people you should always clean up your energy and take it with you when you leave. This applies when you leave other people's homes, but also when you have been to sports practice or in school so you do not just fly out of the door without checking whether you have got everything with you.

You can compare it to being a good and attentive guest who will always help to clear the table when he is visiting other people, so that family and friends or the friends' parents don't have to clear the table for him.

Keeping control of your energy when you are with other people means that it will be easier for you to get your daily energy account to balance, so nobody else will have to do things for you.

Thanks for your time

We believe it is every parent's responsibility to ensure that you youngsters understand and experience how so many things are connected in the real world, when you are old enough to understand this. This depends, of course, on how much knowledge your parents have about these things. Obviously, however, their main task in life is to guide you in living your life in the best way possible and to help you to find suitable solutions to the problems that you keep running up against during your formative years. After all, it is they who chose to put you in the world.

On the other hand, we know that not many parents or other adults have such deep insight into the energy connections as we have described them in this energy guide. So we highly recommend that you share the things you have read in this book with your parents, unless they have already read the book themselves, in which case you might like to share your experiences with each other.

Many thanks for reading this book and we hope to meet you again sometime soon :o)

And what now?

Start using the knowledge you have gained here in your everyday life. Even though you may have a little trouble remembering it at first, gradually it will become quite natural for you to sort out your energy. It can actually reach the point that you become annoyed with yourself if you forget to do it, because it often leads to some stupid problems which could easily have been avoided. So **always** remember to sort your energy!

And if you would like, feel free to help others acquire the same knowledge and insight that you have now, by giving this book as a different kind of gift to a good friend, or to your girlfriend or boyfriend, or to a family member. The more people around you who know about energy sorting, the better it will be for everyone.

If you are curious and would like to know more, please feel free to look at our websites to see what other interesting books and articles we have written.

We also organize courses, which your parents would certainly enjoy taking part in:

www.sennovpartners.com

www.annisennov.eu (books & articles)

www.fourelementprofile.eu (courses)

www.good-adventures.com (publishing)

We also recommend that you read this book

The Little Energy Guide 1
Take care of your own energy

Anni & Carsten Sennov

CPSIA information can be obtained at www.ICGtesting.com
Printed in the USA
BVOW09s2134021114

373287BV00017B/119/P